Love
Facets

Love Facets

EARL BLUE III

To order additional copies of this book, contact:
Xlibris
1-888-795-4274
www.Xlibris.com
Orders@Xlibris.com
553230

Contents

TABLE CUT

The table facet is the largest diamond facet.
Located at the very top of the diamond, the table
often contributes to a large percent of a diamond's
brilliance and fire. Here is where light enters
and exits the diamond - and once the light enters
it reflects and refracts off the other facets.

The first part of the diamond that is seen by the eye
is the 'Table'. The part the all fall in love with in the
store and the most prominent feature of a diamond. I
attribute that first time feeling to be the same when you
first see that someone who starts your heart to racing
and sets your emotions into overdrive.

--- EARL

1

I Miss You

I miss the smell of your hair after
a cold November rain;

I miss the menacing look of anger,
when you are mad at me again.

I miss holding you close to me in the hour of your need;

I miss touching you on the stomach,
while you protected my seed.

I miss your comforting warmth
next to me lying in the bed;

I miss the gentle softness of your fingers
as you rub my aching head.

I miss seeing your frustration as
you crinkle your little nose;

I miss the tingling sensation, when
I kiss you, I get in my toes.

I miss hearing your beautiful laugh
in the morning when I wake;

I miss the sacred times we share
together, walking by the lake.

All these things I miss make your
love invaluable to me;

That is why I will keep you in my
heart and always miss you,

wherever I may be.

First Sight

She is beautiful as the snowcapped mountains.

*Her looks warm the coldest of hearts
and make malice undone.*

I glimpsed her reflection in a silver pool.

Not knowing I could withstand such grace.

Mind, body, soul all rest in one place.

*Her golden mold of creation is
broken again, never used.*

I tremble with the thought, love lost and gone cold.

Let Me Be Your Blanket

I watch you through windowpanes
frosted by the cool autumn wind.

The velvet night sky sprinkled with
diamonds, reflective in your eyes.

Shadows from the fireplace dance
decadently around you.

I'm envious of the intimacy they share.

Welcomed with a kiss, your smile overwhelms me.

Such radiance can eclipse the sun.

I caress your cheek bronzed by the glow of the fire.

As the day's exertion dissolves, the
essence of your beauty revealed.

I watch as you slumber peacefully, unable
to steady my quivering heart.

Holding you close makes me thankful I'm by your side.

I feel you shiver beneath silky satin sheets.

I pull you closer to ease the night's chill.

Beautiful

There is nothing more beautiful
than a woman with child

and the feeling of unity waking up
to her heart-warming smile.

The radiant glow of her complexion
she acquires at noon,

how her eyes shimmer like diamonds
prism by the moon.

How soft and tender her skin has become

making ready her touch to comfort daughter or son.

The fullness of her belly with the growing of our child,

who, hearing the response from her
voice, is sustained for a while.

Her simple worries of looking ugly and
too big can be easily put to rest,

as you comfort her and endearingly
hold her closely to your chest.

Time strengthens the eternal bond
between child and mother,

and it helps her to know that you will
love them both, together and forever.

Entwined

My thoughts are of you.

Your body's softness is a mold to my arms.
Closeness of your breath on my shoulder syncopates my existence,

making you my lifeline.

If severed, so shall end my purpose for living.

I can't see any other way to make it in this world without you.

I lose all desire to seek life with someone else if it means I lose the one true person in my life that makes me complete...

you.

Curves

Road signs warn of dangers ahead.

Cautions ignored at the curves in my bed.

Slippery when wet, apply gently your brakes.

Increased speed through the tunnel, sliding on skates.

Slow down sharp turn ahead,

Approaching NASCAR speeds around curves under my spread.

> *Speed bumps jerk and scrape the undercarriage when we first start.*

> *Mounds and valleys cast shadows, released from a constrictive bra.*

> *Navigation needed to avoid traffic and busy side streets.*

Searching by candle light, no crevasse probed, considered too deep.

Tire tread grips the track with a steady purpose.

Like decadent fingers exploring every inch of every surface.

> *My destination is ahead, right there on the right.*

> *My destination is your curves in my bed tonight.*

Tears

Don't cry love.

If you do, wait till you're in my arms.

*Then a baptism holier than Christ
can my blessing become.*

Allow them to cleanse me washing away my faults.

Caressing my soul and cleansing my thoughts.

Don't cry love.

For then I'd give chase.

*To capture those valuable diamonds and hoard
them as treasure my personal indulgence, held collected,
in the purest of crystal vase.*

*Once the vase is full, ill freeze them complete,
and display them in sunlight, to cast rainbows of color,
never before seen.*

Don't cry love.

For knowing you are.

Makes the pain I feel, unbearable to resolve.

Don't cry my love. Please, don't cry.

*For my heart is yours, only yours,
even if not by your side.*

Lil Love

My ability to love is because you showed me what it is to love.

My happiness is in knowing I have you to come home to and hold.

I have blessings beyond measure and you're the most valuable.

I try many ways to match your love for me but it's difficult to match your perfection.

I laugh.

I'm never going to match your perfection.

I do know I love you and all you do but I'm mostly happy that you say you love me too!

CROWN CUT

The crown of a diamond is the part of the diamond from the girdle up - including the table. Diamonds with a deep cut tend to have higher crowns whereas shallow cut diamonds have very small crowns.

The "getting to know you stage" is the fun part of a relationship. Depending on how it's viewed, it can be a positive outcome or a negative one. Here at the 'Crown' any blemishes made will detract from the overall beauty of a relationship.

---EARL

I Hate Women

Look at them laughing.
Their captivating smiles enfeeble my soul.
I despise their aroma.
Perfumes of Aphrodite saturate my nostrils.
I don't want to see them.
Voluptuous curves that beckons to my loins.
Thinking for themselves.
Invigorating conversations cause my mind to wobble.
Screeching bellows of a hag.
Angelic voices that rattle me to the bone.
Prolific child bearers.
A beautiful package that brings forth life.

You Don't Know What Love Is

If love is given to you, will you keep it in a box?

*Will you put it inside your closet
and keep it under lock?*

Will you plant it and nurture it helping it to grow?

*Or, would you smother it like a burning
ember extinguishing the subtle glow?*

*Would you appreciate the colors of love
that change with the seasons?*

*Probably not, you think for love to be
seen, there must be a reason.*

*How about telling love the truth? Is
that something you could do?*

*Could you share everything with love
that love shares with you?*

*How about saying a few kind words
to show how much you care?*

*I think not, the last time love was around;
you didn't know it was there.*

*I know you don't know what love
is, it clearly can be seen.*

*I've given you love a million times but
you've never given it to me!*

My Words Mean Nothing

Her eyes are deaf to what I'm saying...

Lost the movement of my hands across hers, the noise of my embrace;

a constant buzz only muffled by the stillness of my heart.

With every rise and fall of my chest, its regular pattern resembles wings of butterflies in a rabble.

As I gaze into her eyes, the sound ricochets off the chambers of her heart as if emanating from Pope Sixtus IV architecture; echoes vast and resounding.

She falls...

Not into the dark abyss of Dante but into my empty arms.

They form seamlessly around her supple body. The rigid snapping of sinew as my grasp softens to her every curve is blinding, yet by her, unseen.

Cacophonies of emotions push forward. Damn Hoover, hold them at bay!

Yet, her eyes still do not hear....

My words linger in the air on filaments of silk, hung with the skill of a seamstress seasoned with experience and dedication.

Incus and Malleus transcribes their dull connotation, twins unable to see my true meaning.

I push against her pull as she pulls away; I lay gasping and flushed as the deluge of ecstasy cascades over her. Her pinned up aggression collected between her scapulae is removed and replaced with ease and tranquility.

Love need not reside here; it's still too noisy to see...

I envelope her total being: her eyes can't hear!

I choose her company: her eyes can't hear! I engage in conversation: her eyes,

cannot,

will not,

shall not hear!

So now, instead of me screaming for her reluctant blindness to be removed; I shall write her a letter.

Not with quill and papyrus, but with sentiment and desire.

Then, yes then; will her eyes see the love I have shown through my actions since the beginning.

Questions

Is it better to have loved and lost than to love at all?

Is it better to live life to the fullest, when no one's there to soften your fall?

Can the flavor of life be bittersweet when all you taste is sour?

Does the smell of a rose get better with time or is it lost over the hours?

Can the stillness of a heart in love ever beat again or does the silence of that quivering heart mean that death is close at hand?

Are fields of white lilies and blue lilacs as romantic as they seem?

When deep beneath them both the worms and bugs slither in between?

Can the silver lining of ominous clouds become tarnished with age?

Will the remembrance of amusement park melodies cause hatred and rage?

Alas, if the first loser of a race gets silver and the second loser a bronze, can the looser of this thing called love receive something to hang his looser heart on?

As bold majestic mountains stand against the rain; can love too, be bold as to anchor against the tides of pain?

If so, then love truly must conquer all, but how?

When love has no way of fighting and at the sight of struggle, it goes deaf to your longing call.

It was once said, "Greater love hath no man than this that a man lay down his life for friends."

In the instance when lovers stop being friends is that where life again begins?

The illusion of love escapes me for I see clearly as the dawn; however, is it the invisible strength of love consoling me with the strength to carry on?

Maybe.

Maybe not.

Yet this I know is true, it isn't better to have loved and lost, because the love I lost is you.

Guarded Smile

I see you everyday but say nothing.

*I know that you have pain in your
heart but won't let it go.*

*My friends say I should talk to you
but I don't know what to say.*

*There are times that you seem happy
but it's never on display.*

I talked to you and it felt good. I'm glad I did.

*We had dinner together and I discovered
why you hold on to your pain.*

I asked you if you were scared and you said not of me.

Then I saw what I hadn't seen in a while...

a release of your guarded smile.

Butterflies

On monarch's wings, my stomach quivers.

A guise played out in pain.

Her touch intensifies my shudders, her thoughts catapults this feeling into a sensation I like to feel again.

Strange this fixation deep within, as her explanation amuses; A vexed sensation, a love sensation, but never before used.

    I try and discern the value of these emotions, the fluttering in my soul.

It's as if I'm falling, waiting for the stop at the end. It never comes.

    For the wings that she gives me catch the convections from the abyss and lift me to her waiting

arms and she envelops me as if to never let go again.

        I hold her too.

The way she feels, melts my heart and she then molds it to her liking.

    I find myself lying down, back exposed and trembling beneath her. Her presence beside me, unseen, yet I know she's there as her warmth condenses the air between us making the thought of leaving her unbearable.

I glance in her direction, stealthy and undetected as if stealing a glimpse of her beauty would seal me in a Gorgons kiss. The closeness of her breath collects on my neck and shoulders, causing tingles in slow progression, the fluttering in me still persist.

I relinquish myself to her whims; I give myself to her embrace, her love my chrysalis. I'm her creation this new feeling of expression. She gives me the ability to fly. Lifelessness was I inching along. Now, I'll be free for her and gaze on the world from above.

GIRDLE CUT

The girdle is the widest point of the diamond. Some girdles on diamond cuts are almost non-existent while others have tiny faceted edges that help to increase brilliance and fire. Girdles can affect the grade and quality of the diamond.

Love and hate can be separated by the thinness of boundaries. The 'Girdle' is such a place on a diamond. The separation that this facet gives can mean the difference in a diamond of high quality or quality that's just average. My 'Girdle' is where relationships are pushed right up to the boundary and can be pushed right over it.

      ---EARL

Cheaters Prayer

Heavenly Father:

Remove my sight the cause of my desire.

*The pain of wanting things I cannot
have I will no longer require.*

*If my sight is removed deafen my
ears so no sound am I aware.*

*No voice or sound with nothing to
hear relieves me from care.*

*Aromatic fragrance of her perfume saturates
the nostrils and within my loins a fire ignites.*

*These senses too remove dear God so
I may slumber in the night.*

*The softness of her skin in my embrace
no longer can I withstand.*

*This sensation shall I not need if
no longer I had my hands!*

A kiss full of passion is the last desire left.

*The taste of her forever in me as we
exchanged lover's breath.*

*I have no need for this either my Lord
because alas it stirs my soul.*

*I desire to be rid of her lest I lust again
dear God and totally lose control.*

Cheating

There are many ways to do it, one
needn't know just how.

I didn't think it possible. One day,
unexpectedly, found out.

She was a beautiful Asian girl; who
at first glance I was hooked.

The lust that brewed in my heart, although
I tried, knew it couldn't be shook.

I told my wife all of eight years that
it always took two to tango.

Unbeknown to me that at that moment
I would learn to dance the tango.

At first was bliss. Is this what I miss,
committing to just one lover.

If it is the case then I must chase another and another.

I played the role of single life, went
shopping and club dancing.

I played the role with my wife, raising
children and romancing.

It was easy at first, playing both roles,
one complimented the other.

At times the joy felt was so good, I
thought of telling my mother.

I'd come home from work, find time with the kids.

I wouldn't touch my plate.

All the while deep down inside I'd be
planning that nights date.

I kept it up, paid no attention to the
signs. Soon I was to be caught.

Then it happened while I was nappin'
pictures found not store bought.

Think of a lie! I tried and I tried
but sleep wouldn't leave me.

Maybe I can plan a great escape and
it'll all blow over by evening.

I opened my eyes for now I knew this
dream wasn't me dreaming.

Because I got caught! Damn I was stupid!
Thinking I'd get away with cheating.

LOVE LIE

You say it freely, ease of the wind.

Possibilities endlessly released from within.

Your consolation understood but unseen through eyes,

only your heart can perceive your vision's disguise.

Touching and caressing my facial features;

scrutinizing desire to care for this creature.

Lost to me words of compassion

Depth of your emotions comparable to Mariana.

Reciprocation given at my leisure,
equivalent but unjust.

Reciprocation give unto Caesar equivalent to lust.

Passions I own, but not for you.

Desires I own, but not for you.

Affections I own, but not for you.

Yet in private I portray them with adoration and zeal.

Credit to you my imposition...

your belief is my only thrill.

Cheating
(The Second Time)

Saying I'm sorry helped me to make
it through that last torment.

I went before God; I wrench out my
heart, I hid my face to repent.

I caused needless pain and suffering
to occur in both my mate and I;

I've learned my lesson assigned value
to it, no more will she cry.

But wait...

Trust regained and vows renewed but
duty calls to leave from her site,

The time has come for the ultimate test;
a veil of evil shackles my life.

Satin's plow runs deep and wide
for the seeds he will sow.

I have voices in my head that talk to me,

"What I do she'll never know."

This time love flourished, I couldn't
believe I really lost my head.

Times I'd think: "What am I doing?"
dismiss it and off to bed.

A soul lost forever residing in pain
and dark suppression.

Baptist born, repent last time. Needed
this time: complete confession.

She reminded me how sweet life
could be more than before.

Dreams and infatuations filled my
soul and seeped from my pores.

The pleasure to walk and talk lifted
me, I longed for it to last.

Then reality hit, again I'm spent.

Vulnerable and exposed to lust's formidable grasp;

I did love her. I thought I did

but that feeling, however fleeting,
vanished on thought of my kids.

It was time to leave...

One

I have one, but don't want it.

I love it, but don't feel it.

I had one, but lost it, so I'm looking for one but still need it.

If I could trade one, I would do it. I know where there is one, but can't pursue it.

I want the same one, but scared to do it.

I asked for one and hope that one chooses.

One left me for another one. (That one hurt), I left one for another one, which no one deserved.

I see one everyday knowing not, if that one, a good one will make.

I settle for one, the original one, that one I feel safe.

I just want one that is one but want my present one. I know there isn't one better than that one...

I've looked.

There's no one that can replace that one.

Still I want one.

Self

I loose it every time I journey to the outside of life precious existence.

Innocence no longer matters; it's a notion that no longer matters.

As I laid my remorse on the alter—twice; I found myself picking them up again devoid of any true absolution.

Really?

Can no other joy be given without agony and pain?

Can the one true unadulterated, unequivocal, shameless, blameless, pivotal, consummated love exist?

I've looked into the mirror only to see the empty orbs of a man whose futile pursuits have led him down the road of total damnation, a road that has been his alone.

I've looked into his soul and found the hatred and contempt for self. He has forever held it in his grasp. He engulfs its bitter taste and relishes it.

His ever longing desire for more consumed the purest thought as bile dissolves the contents of his ingestion.

He is a Symbiote, thriving in the degradation of those around him.

Yet as the removal of this poison begins, his demeanor reverts to a vile and decrepit shell filled with pitted emotions and careless actions.

I turn away...with only hope as my refuge.

PAVILION CUT

The pavilion of a diamond includes the lower
portion of the diamond from the girdle down.
Again, in some cuts the pavilion can be quite
deep and in others it is very shallow.

Deep emotional scars from relationships can be seen
physically and are the embodiment of what is used in
someone's makeup. Remembering the pain and not
living the pain is the goal of all who are damaged. The
'Pavilion' does just that to a diamond refracting light
throughout the body of the diamond.

  ---EARL

Demons

I chase the ghost of my past never to see an end.

My demons own me, my perpetual sin.

I know I have a savior, who washed them away.

I had those blessings and those penances,
but those I threw away.

I chase endlessly thinking I have time,

But my journey returns me again to the starting line.

Try as I will, to stop, I look for help, but the
devils outstretch hand is all that's there.

(I'm looking in the wrong places)

I see the familiar faces, those that lie with their
greeting, but it's me that's lying, my demons are
lying, looking for women that aren't completing.

I sulk in the corner, never to be whole.

I writhe in pain with the thoughts
of losing eternally my soul.

I've overcame passion and desire, with fear and dread,
only to find Satan's succubus a companion in my bed.

I hate my demons but feed to their needs, their
controlling and owning, unceasing with their greed.

(I call on Him for help)

*I leave my skin on the surface of the
counter, this alter made from bone.*

*I look for another sacrifice, but it's my blood that
quenches the thirst. Mine, and mine alone!*

*I've faltered in my endeavor to reach my
dismal goal, to have three consorts equal in
nature living as one, complete and whole.*

*Although I've dabbled, unknowing to those
in who played, making it a fact of life
leave me disfigured and dismayed.*

*Two cells joined to make one, also I desired, but finding
one that was able, my demons them too devoured.*

*My seeking is no longer my yearning,
and my yearning I no longer seek.*

*Ill forever basks in the tumultuous sea of regret,
filled with tears that I constantly weep.*

Shadows of happiness lost, now my only vice.

*Blood stained attempts to remove them from
my mind, saturate the covers of my bed.*

*Cast aside the scars of turmoil, which
cover my body, from toes to head.*

The end of life a gambit, I alone choose to play.

*No one shall miss me, yet I feel I'm
missing, a Wilson cast away.*

(my demons love me)

I change my view, marring a gift to me presented.

Lord forgive me, this gift I received,
uncouth and not loved,

I have not represented the best of your
will and pretend to be from above.

Examples you've given me, yet
seeing them I refuse to tell.

I'll find my eternal damnation, soliloquy with those
burning regressions deep within the bowels of hell.

Got Away

I cry at the thought of how I lost her... should I pursue her hoping my life's box of second chances isn't empty or allow her happiness to continue without me? My pain without her is my punishment for the way I treated a treasure as she.

Will my pursuit of her allow me the happiness and the love I long for knowing such happiness will come at the lost of my current joy; or will I again succumb to the angst of loss, this now my present situation.

This two fold am I. My fortuitous life and my unambiguous pain, both which I have only a fraction of the contentment I had with her.

I have but a shadow of pure joy, which if her company pursued, I know I would feel again even unto fleeting friendship of acquaintance.

I wrench at my weathered soul in search of the origin of this pain; only to find the fermented bile of a husk, bearing a keen resemblance of a man; only her love and touch can again animate this form and until it does, if ever, forever dead I will remain.

I Loved

I loved her but failed and let her go.

I choose another, who thus became my foe.

A smile on me she generates on sight, I again yearn to have her by my side.

I lost my soul when she left my life. To me she's a partner, a friend, a wife.

Her compassion for my happiness surpassed what I was able to feel.

My sadness at her departure makes for my torture, cast forever in Death's shadowy fields.

I loved.

I'm Scared to show trueness in all my endeavors.

A genuine lack of emotion shrouded her, my guilty pleasure.

I wanted her forever, relentless to let her know.

I lost the best thing to happen to me; now I'm scorned emotionally never to grow.

Happiness never again shall I feel because I loved: remorse, torment, pain my companions.

Medals displayed on my heart like a champion, eternal gifts bestowed from above.

I loved.

I'm excited to see three faces of joy.

They too lost to me, two girls one boy.

We played tag on bars made for monkeys, what excitement is this?

A mother's voice ignored at dangers remiss.

Back and forth heart strings are pulled; I lost the tug-o-war.

It's three against one but whose keeping score?

I want those smiles from All Hollows Eve. Ghoulish Zombies and Ghastly Princess pleasing yet shudders my entire being.

Gone is the joyous clamor of days spent with me, a deafening silence multiplied by three.

I LOVED.

I patiently wait; for her to return? No.

I Lost her; with only festering scars to show.

I wait, my ability to heal lost to time.

My bandages come from the tattered memories in my mind.

Again I dream to have her in my arms; a fleeting thought I'm always hopin'.

Holding on to this Inception helps me survive a terminal notion.

I loved. I loved. I loved. Yes it's very possible... I Loved.

Waterfalls

Waterfalls are falling yet again. Welcome pain, my long lost friend.

I tried again to look beyond, only to find happiness once there, removed and gone.

I'll console myself in the mist of my transgressions, insanity my only lesson. To come so far this time with a gal in reach, I leave yet again pedestal empty and incomplete.

So into the depths of love I myself find, an abyss of lost and tattered souls.

Interest cashed in and lost to time, a heart frozen and forever cold.

Last Shred

I look at it daily, the letter written on a scrap piece of paper.

Just twenty-one simple words give me meaning and inspiration.

Through anguish and torment we sailed together on the restless sea of love, but my solace from this simple life came not from above.

It was as my beacon of hope a sign of boisterous happiness forthcoming in my years.

Now it's a symbol of dread gloom invoking nothing but tears.

My life had purpose, filled with direction and true meaning.

All these notions dissipated as wisps of fog rolling over riverbanks in the evening.

I wipe away my tears; no more crying is needed for this pain.

I reflect as to how this started that lone and fateful day about noon:

(Redacted)Don't forget me! I love you so much baby and ill be seeing you real soon!

I love you!

(<3) (Redacted)

This Too Shall Pass

I said bye for the last time with a heart in pieces. Love no longer a goal I seek. May the pain be removed from me forever, happiness within myself. I am my new lover.

-Words of the insane Love Seeker

I've given what I can and it wasn't enough. In the end it was tough to see you walk away knowing I'll never hold you again.

Last I cried...

Last I lied...

Last I laughed...

Last I tried.

Pain again my friend and my foe a stinging reminder of things I used to know.

Adolescent descent into relationship squandered; yet, still as an adult I must ponder.

Does love even exist with the intent of happiness?

Is it like existential dreams, a universe of lifeless, nothingness?

She asked for more of my time, I lost my watch.

She asked for more love, I lost my heart.

She asked me stay the night, I left at midnight.

Now I again find myself at the end of this road, looking over my shoulder.

Forever, looking over my shoulder.

Secrets

I told her something from my mind, I almost lost her.

There are other secrets I hold deep
inside, telling her now; ridiculous!

I'm not going through the drama twice!

A daily game I play with myself,

I play spy in my home and the target is self.

I pick and choose the information,
voluminous tomes explored.

I shift through shelves in my mind,
many new creases I explore

I love her very much and don't
desire to hurt her again.

Yet, the things I keep from her;
makes her forever my friend.

My secrets don't get told, they are
mine to keep till my grave.

I tell no one their composition; many are
mine but others I did not make.

Holding on to the idea that peace can
be everlasting with silence,

I laugh when I'm inquired to divulge
with the utmost of passion.

*I have said some things that made
others think about my intentions.*

*Keeping her protected and from the darkness
my soul has, my current mission.*

Questions I deflect to a different existence,

*only to find the deflection look back
from the morning mirror.*

*I cry daily from the deception
thinking my life will get better.*

A life of secrets with regrets as their partner in dance,

*my vocals silenced, losing her with
revelations, an untaken chance.*

I paid with my soul to live in this pit of refuse.

I mortgage of eternity with no minimum due.

*Content in my decision to hold this vile
tongue, only one of which I posses,*

With dreams of admiration, that one day,

*I can remove this albatross of secrets
from the crux of my chest.*

Alone

Sitting here, looking at pictures from days before, while rain cascades silently down my door.

Memories faded, again renewed.

Ghost and shadows of butterflies flutter back in view.

Oppressed emotions begin to stir in the bowels of sins long past.

Emotions of the highest degree bring regret closer to my grasp.

I shun the notion with disgust. I know my place in time.

If He would allow it, to part with the present, in the past she would have been mine.

I'm Tired of Smiling

I'm tired of hiding the pain of my heart.

I just want one to be apart,

No reason for the lie to continue.

I just want to be the only one with you.

I've had the chance of feeling the unjust,

I've even been the reason for mistrust.

But I can no longer smile.

Heaven has open the flood gates and poured out blessings unworthy.

Hell has opened its brimstone pits and accepted me with arms deserving.

Chastising me by fire and not allowing me the ease of retribution.

Lo, through it all, I'm shone a glimpse of happiness, a sliver of hope but now, no longer can I smile.

My heart is heavy.

  My heart is heavy.

    My heart is heavy.

I Never Knew You

I never knew you as we talked that late afternoon.

You chatted me up such a delightful tune.

I had been in places unseen and dark.

Never to see the light of day with this cold shriveled heart;

I've been beaten and trodden upon, a penance of my own creation;

floundering in the steadfast grip of insanity my endless revolutions in perfect syncopation.

For as soon as I think I'm surfacing for that life saving breath of fresh air,

another relationship ends in damnation and my eternal despair.

But I never knew you

I never held you after a night of love making.

I never smelled you in the kitchen breakfast making.

I never kissed you in clothes drench by an April rain.

I never listened to you just to ease your pain.

All this time, we've talked and laughed through the electronic age.

I even cry as if I had you to loose as I type on this page.

Laughing manically at the ill fated chance to be happy and free;

again I'm writing at the loss of love a new cycle of my irrationality.

But I never knew you

One door closes, the other is locked.

The key lies within your heart which is also the lock.

I've faulted in my divulgence, a calculated risk,

only to be shunned and cast aside as fodder served on a cold silver dish!

Mistakes I have made in the seeking of another as mine while entwined with one present;

but, this my only desire since the early thought of its mental conception.

Yes I never knew you.

Because as I lay here thinking of what could have been instead of what will be,

I lay here thinking of what is and never shall become.

Longing

I see her every day, I am such a fool, to have dismissed such a jewel, into the abysmal pool, for another to use.

I long for her return, to extinguish an ember that still burns, hard lessons I had to learn, wishing again for another turn, forever shall I yearn.

A simple misunderstanding, a life duplicitously demanding, her request too commanding, nightly residuals constant asking, life together never was lasting.

Jealously at her kissing another, my future kid's mother, causing my soul to shudder, yet I dare not udder, hole in my heart replaced by no other.

In passing we give a glance, with her I knew romance, please cupid give me another chance, it's too lonely in this chamber to dance, I regret love's happenstance.

It will linger with me forever, a happiness unbridled with simple pleasures, blessings twice removed endeavors, limp my egress stagger, and she dismisses me like I don't matter.

I feel resentment and scorn, love shallow and unborn, a testament forlorn, from within her discourse words torn, my true sentiments forgone.

Chide of her embellished laughter, amongst peers plots my character's disaster, she equivocates my soul into plaster, as the meaning of our kiss in her mind, no longer lasted.

Replacement

*I think I may have a new and
significant, totally awesome,*

*unadulterated, unequivocal, hands
down, but put them*

*back up just in case, opposite of a
negative but also a positive...*

Replacement!!!!!

The first time I faltered. The second time I cried.

This time it's simple and easy, I'm so glad I tried.

Milk gets spilled, dropped, leaked or poured out.

As long at the jug isn't dry, you can get a...

Replacement!!!!!

I have two hands to hold you.

I have two eyes to see you.

I have two legs to come to you.

I have two lips to kiss you.

*If you damage one of these this of
which I have two, ill still be ok.*

I only have one heart, if damaged there's no...

Replacement!!!

CUTLET CUT

*This is the very bottom facet of a diamond,
and it is only located on diamonds which
come to a pointed tip at the bottom.*

*The reality of how love hurts is very prominent in
relationships and is sharp enough to cut deeply leaving
irreparable damage. The 'Cutlet' is the point that can cut
glass but is also the place where the weight of the entire
diamond sets and also rounds out the completeness and
beauty we all love.*

---EARL

Trust

You said this, but did that.

You did this, but said that.

Your actions are the words that resonate with me.

Your words are the actions that deceive me.

It's the custom of your nature to be misleading.

For this reason, I cease my pleading.

Your whims and your quirks are founded in deceit, a flaw love cannot overlook.

I feel the sting of neglect, your expression passionless and incomplete, as half-eaten bait still on a hook.

I remove myself from the Amber color of jealously less it consumes my soul.

Rivers cried from blood shot eyes renewed floodwaters for crimson seas.

I need not worry whose company you keep or, what you are doing anymore.

Your boisterous words now fall silent on ears deaf from apologies.

No more!

A seething sickness from within my gut disgorges itself stained with blood.

Your face is featureless, drawn from immeasurable distances

a span even too far for love.

I shudder with thought of your inconsistencies and intolerable acts, which your love tries to explain.

I am no longer your prisoner, frozen with thoughts of loosing you, forever lobotomized from my brain.

I am as careless to you as a leaf to the wind, a futile resistance most vain.

My trust in you has crumbled, dust beneath my feet, lifeless in its reminder of forgotten passion,

life without you, now complete; freedom from a parasitic attraction.

December 21st 2010

Here I sit quietly with tears in my eyes, mourning the loss of love.

I finally found the place where she resides and wish the address was lost to me forever.

I had no intentions of finding her, yet; I sought feverishly for her.

I had no thought of finding her because until she came to me, I wasn't for her.

This incessant confinement of an emotion from within my soul causes me to grieve deeply.

The constant reminder of something I had.

I don't know if the yearning for her return will ever leave me. Can I find her again? Do I want to?

All I know is it is a paralyzing feeling when you lose this thing call love.

No one should have to go through this amount of pain.

Morphine could not stem the intolerable cruelty that has me in tears.

To mourn the death of something so endearing has no way of quailing the suffering felt by an aggressor without form or hands.

An attacker who I am powerless to combat but yet has struck such a fatal blow so as to have killed me with one strike of her mighty hand.

Love I curse thee, for no more do I want to feel the wrath which you bring! I curse thee for as long as I have sought you, your cunning and willingness has kept you aloof from my grasp.

Now after all these years, after a many of travels around the world, through countless relationships and countless trials and errors, I find you! I wish you dead and never to find you again.

Death of the Butterflies

Feelings never before felt at the touch of your hand.

Fingers delicately manicured and trimmed, trace the path goose pimples follow as if lead by a Pied Piper.

No one has touched me so...

Softness of your lips excites as well as entice.

Your kiss soaks all sensations of my being into parted lips longing for the taste of yours.

If for a moment, I feel nothing, yet... I feel everything.

Mind engulfed with thought of being with you.

The thoughts I have shudders my soul with the reverence of the Holy Spirit.

These sensations no longer shall I feel.

The Butterflies are dead!

I miss the feelings you introduce to me that cold November night. The urges I would get while looking at you through a drunken sight. Thinking to myself will this spasm linger in my belly forever and a day. But once you explained it to me, I wanted more of it to my dismay. The cringes I felt at the sight of your beauty, similar to the bends. The foremost of my pleasure from you, separated from friends.

Then it happed. You departed from me, as a ghost on the wind.

Gone from me in earnest no more

Words

Your words remove my skin with the skill of a surgeon, but even the finest sword ever crafted dulls when put against time, so too do your words become dull with their constant use.

So continue to...

Ridicule,

Slander,

Mock,

Chastise,

Bombard,

Inject,

and pummel me.

I am no longer allowing your...

Dull,

Blunt,

Drab,

Obtuse,

Lifeless,

words to again use my mind or body as their sheath!

Anger

*I have neither resolve to live like a king nor any
desire to live with a poisonous, bitter, shell that's
empty and won't allow repair. My depiction of self is
sinister and vile; however, my parring with anything
despairing as any of the ominous Sirens vested with
hate and venom who categorize all men with those
from past pains only to relive those pains with each
new encounter, shall no longer be coupled with my
undulating life and drain my happiness like a ghastly
Wraith leaving me to succumb to the dreaded fear of
being left alone and tattered once again.*

*Their harboring of this lingering animosity siphons
all whims of my ever existing in a relationship void
of turmoil and the persecution and causes me to
abandon a perpetual desire to appease all women who
cling to their scorn and disseminate it judgmentally
en masse without discerning the true character of a
current suitor. I attest that most of my pursuits begin
with earnest admiration but then fall as a hallowed
victim to the obligatory ills festering in the minds of
those who I deem worthy of exchange.*

Lo, I am not blind!

*I have considered my contributions in promoting
this ubiquitous flaw and I take blame for my share
but I will not lie in the path of those whose desire
it is to batter and torment all just because their*

feelings are tainted with the angst of rejection or pot marked with actions of love remised never again to be trusted. Those who decapitate with indiscretion at the unconditional retort given to the answer that spews forth from their loins begging for satisfaction. The circumcised expectations ridden with doubt and mistrust that I must prove myself against over and over only to again be swallowed and gnashed with the rhetorical, that for no other purpose, serve to prove the disproven ideas reverberating in their head.

I shudder and quake with the anticipation of retribution given from him who is the only one fit for this cause; yet, I traverse against the earthly judgment daily as to how I am to live. I no longer seek penance here where none abound. No more will I waste my energy in receiving fulfilment.

Love Insane

I chase till I'm tired, no more can I run. Chasing after love, a beaten man I've become. I find walls and barriers constantly in my path. For as one gets close enough it slips gracefully through my grasp.

I return to the beginning.

I chase till I'm tired, no more can I run. Chasing after love, a beaten man I've become. I find walls and barriers constantly in my path. For as one gets close enough it slips gracefully through my grasp.

I return to the beginning.

I chase till I'm tired, no more can I run. Chasing after love, a beaten man I've become. I find walls and barriers constantly in my path. For as one gets close enough it slips gracefully through my grasp.

I return to the beginning...

No More Shall I Fail

I can't give up...no, not now.

This is the point where I usually fail, but not this time.

My success is contingent on my happiness and I refuse to sacrifice it anymore.

Justified in my endeavors by my need to make all attempts in ensuring I have exhausted all avenues of acceptance.

I must ensure that the welfare of my kind is kept intact and my desires do not foreshadow the truest nature I'm able to convey.

Lastly, if I ever deviate from this goal, of which I must obtain, then I shall surely lose all purpose in life and thus resort back into the wretched vile disgusting dilapidated soul from which I have been redeemed. I shall no longer pursue anyone for the lost of this one chance will make all others fail in comparison and foundations of heaven itself will shudder at the failure.

No more shall I fail at happiness!

1000

The shutter clicks.

You here the mumbled disgust of both her and her friend.

The shutter clicks again.

Sniggles and giggles you know its just right, getting up to leave for dinner and enjoy the rest of the night.

You jump to your feet, prepared to leave in just a moment.

The shutter again clicks.

You fall in a heap back on the couch waiting this ridiculous torment. This time their eyes were closed.

Click...

>*Click...*

>>*Click...*

You hear the constant clicking of the phone, a rhythm so frequent; it could be a ring tone.

The time on the clock puts you two hours past late, forty-five of that was keeping the makeup from turning into cake.

You get up to go see why the photoshoot isn't done; only to find out they haven't got the one.

Which one with a bewildered look you ask which one is just right?

Looking at each other and without missing a beat...

>>*the one that will get a thousand likes.*

ROUGH CUT

Rough diamonds are those that are mined,
before they are cut and polished.

Rough, dirty, bumpy and gritty are all ways diamonds
are found. The deep dark cavasses and treacherous
dangers faced to get these stones make the final product
the most valuable in the world. The diamond in the
'Rough' is what shall be the next relationship find in life.

---Earl

REKINDLING

I miss you my love!

My heart aches with emptiness inside.

I have no other desire than to hold you and drink my fill of your essence.

I want to look into your eyes and gaze into eternity.

I want to feel your touch and know that you are mine.

I AM YOURS!

I need you to complete this empty vessel never to have it empty again.

Her

She taught me butterflies can live in the fall.

We had a second floor meeting in a sanitized hall.

Together our social gatherings contained mutual inhibitions.

Tears beget tears, nurturing and developing, growing love's intentions.

Her smile, subtle and beguiling, Da Vinci Lisa's incarnate.

At our first kiss, my lungs life essence into her, did escape.

Her golden locks entangled with my hands.

Fear if I were to lose the, I'd be less a man.

Her will to be mine made my will long to be hers.

Her eyes would meet mine, soothing and secure.

If

If you can't imagine a life without them, keep them.

If you can't imagine a life with them, leave them.

If they do things you never imagined, let them.

If you never imagined you would be with them, accept them.

If you imagined life, as it should be instead of as it is, get real.

If your real life has you imagining your life as it could be, stay real.

If your imagination runs wild, let it.

If you haven't an imagination, get it.

If you're imagining this poem is about imagination your wrong. It's about the word "if", that when used, leaves no imagination to succeed in anything at all.

The Next One

She will have...

...a sensitive attitude, one that's demure yet strong and independent, yielding to suggestions only if prudent. She will be ever sweet and wholesome, one who takes care of self and not uncouth. Her clothes will fit as a comforting silk robe or like a glove. Her decency expressed in every facet of life, like diamonds cut by the finger of God and she'll smell good too. Her eyes will be like pools of artic water covered in moon dust. If I were to fall in, I'd allow myself to succumb to the tendrils of death, knowing I'll forever be a part of her. Her smile will radiate bright enough to clear the darkest night and darkest depths of my heart. Angels will use her laughter as a tuner to their celestial harps and her hair will flow unimpeded like the falls of Niagara. She will have the body of Eve from the dawn of creation and be voluptuous and desirable in all ways.

Yeah the next one will be like this!

Love Lost

He said, "It's better to have loved and lost..."[1] Then what use is love if you lose it at every cost?

It doesn't matter if the pain is held deep within...

just like salt to a wound, when open, it hurts again!

Scantily clad garments protect him from the rain,

aimlessly he wonders, tattered and torn from the pain.

Slowed gait in his walk, with weight of the world on his shoulders...

the love he pursued from her never could be colder.

He reminisces of times full of light laughter, unimpeded hastily going after her;

Placing all after her, including self, subdued reactions at displayed emotions never again felt.

Her tears he console as she hopped from one guy to another, him wanting more, her wanting a brother.

Deep inside he knew the chances was slim but soon abated upon her return to him! Him who hurt her, him who made her cry, him who if he could, would slit his throat and take his life!

---

[1] Alfred Lloyd Tennyson

He would do it... in a min if he knew her happiness would truly be the ending.

You know what they say...

Battle scared and tired from <u>The Art of War</u>, *love like New England running up the score. Wanderer wears his heart on the cuff of his sleeve given only to her who will receive. On albatross wings into her arms he flies thinking he again found love no reason or rhyme. Dual verbal confirmation of life in her womb something they both desired to make happen all too soon. Two turns to three his alone to nevermore. Within her another's seed she bore....*

Yet again wretched with pain and disgust, loves nightmarish dream; only he can trust. Ice syncopates rhythms within his chest deflection for Eros's arrows no need for a vest.

I have loved and have lost my heart being the cost.

Tattered vessel unable to contain love's true intentions my loss,

   battlefield of an empty organ again I toss.

A puerperal crevice gains no advance, forever distorted and maimed.

   Ice interlocking tendrils, comfortable and familiar, solidifying what remnants remain!

A champion deserve, with true intentions perceived; a champion I was, drawn in and deceived.

No longer to remain in an embrace tempered, with mutual passions and desires.

Now I'm a wondering apparition, soulless, seamlessly pacing with the ebb of emotions lingering no more, a man of St. Elmo's fire.

Tired from the incessant pursuit, those captured constantly reject my attempts and get away. Insanely shaken till loosed the hunter now becomes prey. Days of empty nets forevermore, jealously is keeping score.

Choices

I had my choice but chose wrong and the choice I choose; chose to be gone. I'll choose again for the choice is mine but my next choice must be a mutual choice or no choice the next time.

Choosing to loose isn't in my mind, those choices I choose to leave in a past so far behind.

> *I choose to leave them there and not choose them but learn.*

> *If hind sight is 20/20 then my last choice I see clearly and choose to make them my last.*

> *My head's much clearer from the choices I've made, those choices, despicable choices, I choose to leave and keep my head this way.*

> *So for now I choose to be here alone in my thoughts, because to live without choices is not living and I refuse to choose to live as if I was lost.*

Thoughts of Desire

I know one, so I want one.

Had one, but lost it only to find one again.

Saw one and heard one but for me, it was the same one.

Bought one and gave one but never did I receive one.

So I'll hold one to let go of one and sometimes ...ill console one.

I'll match one.

I'll catch one.

Hoping one day... I become one.

Want

Want her badly; you'll find her.
Want her badly enough; she'll find you.
Want only her; she'll be yours too.

Want her, blemishes and perfections.
Want her, ideas and thoughts.
Want her, passions and her discretions.
Want her and she will never have you guessing.

I'll Love Again

Embracing you close enough to see
my reflection in your eyes,

I would look into them as the beauty they contain,

cascades over my soul and I loose myself in their gaze.

Tightly I envelope you in my grasp so
your essence saturates my being,

your rapidly beating heart, sustains
my life as well as yours;

if you were removed from my life I'd surely die.

I gently wisp away a lock of your hair
so to behold the skin of alabaster.

A face molded in Aphrodite's form.

As my lips press against yours, I taste a
sweetness of honey, pure and unrefined.

I only stop such a sweet kiss after my thirst for
this addiction is quenched and satisfied.

My hands desire your flesh, removing your
shirt to expose the softness of your skin.

The excitement fills you as you
quiver beneath my touch.

I untie your loosely clasping robe and
watch as it gathers at your feet.

I stand in awe, as the candlelight
illuminates your body.

I'm jealous of the flames as they get first taste of you.

I rush in to embrace you, fearing I may fall

This is feeling of bliss, if only could
last forever, is yours to own.

A complete release of my cares and
my fears you have bestowed

on me without care.

Agony no more, tears abated, new
life given to a heart long dead,

new found beginnings all because of you.

Inspiration

I missed you at first sight but was happy to be you blanket as we entwined.

I hated women thinking they didn't know what love was.

Your curves are the most beautiful things I love about you, it's a lil love filled with questions and this love won't lie.

I fight tears constantly in the presence of your guarded smiles; as if I alone am chasing butterflies to save them, right before they die.

Trust I have of you makes the choices of my words easy to express my thoughts of desire, rekindling my longing for you as if it was December 21st 2010.

I remember you thought my words meant nothing, as if all I wanted was the last shred of your secrets.

You thinking my love were a lie because you saw me with one girl.

I never knew you then and I didn't care for her. I was never seen cheating and never had love lost but I have failed at it.

Making you my next one, a permanent replacement, no more shall I fail.

So for you, I'll insanely love you and make it cascade over you like a 1000 waterfalls and if you let me wash away those angry demons of the past two cheaters that got away... ill love again.

Made in the USA
San Bernardino, CA
04 March 2017